HOWLING AT THE MOON

Howling at the Moon

Darshana Suresh

PLATYPUS PRESS, England

ISBN 978-1-9997736-4-9

Second Edition, 2018

Cover and interior layout by Peter Barnfather
Type set in Bergamo Pro, FontSite Inc.

Published by Platypus Press

to the moon, for always coming back

to my parents, for never leaving

ONE

TWO

THREE

ONE

Birds on a Power Line

How much can you tell me about love?
Enough to fill my breakfast bowl.
And what can you tell me about it?
Have you ever touched a jellyfish?
Ever stepped on broken glass at the beach?
Does it hurt that much? No, no.
No, you misunderstand—
I only meant to say that it fills your
mouth with blood. *So, it hurts.*
A little, but I hurt more without it.
Oh? Tell me about the Not Love, then.
Must I? It makes my bones crack
and my marrow spill out—

[…]

Alright, if you insist. It's like being
held under the water except there
is no water, just ice, just ice and lava
and dead souls floating in the Lethe.
It's like drowning, but there's a wall
and on the other side you can see
people laughing. And breathing. The
hardest part is seeing them breathing.
Okay. Tell me about the Love.
Like stepping into sunlight. Like
catching moonbeams in your hands.
Like your body, floating painlessly.
Warm and glowing and welcoming,

like the earth calling you home with
open arms. Like the relief you feel
when someone pulls that shard of
glass out of your foot. *When was the
last time you felt this—this warmth?*
Uh, well. I don't remember. A while ago.
Weeks. Months. Years. I don't know.
You stop counting when the numbers
become higher than the people who
love you. *So people do love you.* I
guess so. They say they do. *What's
the matter, then?* Nothing. It doesn't
matter. *It should matter. It does matter.*

[laughter, low and bitter]

Alright. It's just—eggshell love. Like
birds sitting on a power line. One misstep
and suddenly, everything is burning.
I don't want to set things on fire anymore.
That's all. That's all.

Pliant

Always opening and closing,
always mouth searching.

Babies have this reflex called
rooting, do you know?
If you stroke their cheek,
they turn towards your hand,
expecting to be fed.
It's meant to disappear at
around four months.

I think—I think I never lost
that. When someone shows me
even the tiniest bit of kindness
my entire soul still twists
towards them. A sunflower
searching for the sun. A
hatchling keening for its mother.

I keep falling (in love) and falling (in love)
and falling (in love). Knees raking the
ground. Standing with blood pooling
around my feet. Still leaping with
outstretched arms. See,

last week this girl smiled at me and
I just thought, *no, no,*
   don't do that, don't,
      I'm weak and broken and wanting
        and I will tie myself around you like a vine.

I will push my body around until it
    fits yours. I will write your name on my veins.
        I will open and and open and

crack right
        down the middle.

Love Is

The mother bird carrying food in her
mouth to her hatchlings despite the hunger
chewing at her own stomach.

Hey, have you reached home safely?

Her staring at you like you hung the stars
in the sky when she thinks you're not
looking. Like the moon is made up
of every breath that leaves your chest.

This reminded me of you.

Your shadow, always returning to your side.

The smell of sunlight / the clocktower
toiling / hands, clasped under the blanket.

Every sunset you watched with tears sliding
down your face. Every sunrise you missed
because you were too happy in your dreams.

Sunflowers.

Your blood clotting / neurones firing /
heart always beating and beating.
Your own hands falling out to catch you
before you hit the ground. All the ways
you save yourself even when you don't want to.

Love is the way your body fights to keep you alive.
Day after day after day.

A Plea from Shaking Knees

Two oceans away, a boy is falling in love.
Next door, another boy is just falling.
One is laughing, one is crying—
both are screaming.

Here is a secret: love comes quietly.
In the dead of night, fingers painted
white, toes curled in anticipation.
Anything else in its place would be
called an intruder, but love makes people
forget their own names, and for some reason
forgetting has become gospel.

Here's another secret: the boy
who is just falling leaves his fingerprints
all over his bedroom wall. Hopes that
at least some part of him survives. That
even if he can't, his body will leave a mark.

Here's another secret: some days I am falling
in love and other days I am just falling.

Here's a bigger secret:
I cannot tell those days apart.

Here's the biggest secret:
I don't want to fall anymore.
I don't want to die.

The Untameable

Tell me about the people you drowned
in the well, how they're all the memories
you try to lock away daily. Tell me about
your lover holding your head in the water,
saying, 'I love you,' despite knowing that
those are the only words that will ever
scare you away.

The pattern of your life goes like this:
you build a home and it burns away and
so you try to follow but even the flames
don't want you. You crawl into someone's
skin and they're so scared of love they
spit you back out again, and so you
wear their fear like a bridal veil.

The memories you drowned (one after
the other, all staring at you with dead
eyes as they sunk under the water)
watch you as if you are an unfinished
story. Your lovers stand in a line by
the wall, their faces a haunting you
can never forget.

Tell me about how no one looks at you
like art so you have learnt to treat
yourself like a masterpiece. And the
pattern of your life goes like this: love /
lose / love / lose / love / love / love.

To You

That when you wake up
your cheeks are dry.
That the sun kisses your

fingertips good morning
& the moon your wrists
goodnight. That when you laugh,
honey gets stuck in the sound.

This is to you.
You, bomb-blast-heart, cratered
with love. You, raindrop so big
you've forgotten what it's like
to be afloat / to be breathing.

You, girl with fishhooks
shredding your lungs.
You, boy with sandstorms
under your skin.
You, person who chased
happiness for so long
you forgot to look for it behind you.

You, the emergency sirens.
You, the reader.

You were always meant to be here.
You were always meant for the sun's
warmth, for the moon's breathless joy.

You, the reader.
Here is a love letter stamped
with your name.
For every second you thought
you wouldn't make it.
For every second you didn't
want to make it.

You made it.
Thank you for existing (so beautifully).

The Body, Hanging on a Nail

And this is what heartbreak
sounds like:

> ocean floors rolling in her stomach,
> the stench of dead fish nauseating /
> overwhelming / sickening.

> Overhead the moon belches and
> falls out of the sky, a giant parachute
> with a puncture wound the size of
> Jupiter, & dust trails in a cloud.

> Heartbreak: a kissing booth with
> a line full of skeletons, their teeth
> rattling / shivering / gnashing.

> Heartbreak: babies lying in their
> cradles, lips moving and hands
> flailing but soundless / careless.

> Your heart? Damned / dammed.

> Heartbreak is a meal you devour
> with hungry fingers, the skeleton of
> a shark that has lost all its teeth.

> Heartbreak is a body, skinless.
> Your heart, loveless.
> The way it always has been.

TWO

There's This Girl

She says she understands.
That when I say I spend whole
days floating above myself
before realising that there's
something wrong, she's
floating right beside me.
Helicopter-blade hearts
ripping each other into pieces.

She asks me how my heart is,
and I say, 'beating.'
That's never the answer you
want, and I'm sorry about that.
I wish the hurt took a break, too.
I'm sorry the pain doesn't come
and go when it's convenient for you.

She understands, though.
Gives me a rubble of rock and
says that it used to be a mountain.
I take it as a metaphor for her smile.

When she says she hasn't cried
in days, her voice trembles in pride.
I do not point out the tear tracks
on her cheeks. I understand
the need to convince others
you're okay before you can believe
it yourself. I understand that
you can never really believe it yourself,

but everything in your body
relies on you trying anyway.

She asks me what I would say
if I could tell anyone anything.
'Stanch this bleeding,' I say.
'Please. I can't handle always
seeing red.'

The next day, her lipstick is pink.

A Lullaby for the Lost and Found

This is how the story goes:
the leaves turn brown and split
from the trees / the flowers rip
themselves apart and shoot petals
to the ground, one after the other.

They call this autumn.
  I call this survival.

This bark chipping.
    This bluebird calling.
      This fingernail bleeding /
skin peeling / stars falling.

I watch the new moon
like it's something holy.
It's the only thing that
understands what I mean
when I say that I want to
    start over.

I talk to the stars and
call each one by your name.
When none of them respond
I convince myself that I'm
just practising for
    your
        leaving.

Every autumn I
      take myself into my arms
   and kiss my palms
for making it through another year.

Every spring, the leaves
turn green again / the
flowers bloom again /
I grow with them.

Again.

Holy

Gaudy high school dance.
Paper decorations, punch,
glitter-smudged cheeks;
the whole set. Silver dress,
gold hair piled up into
    a crown.

So ethereal I was afraid you'd
disappear if I touched you.
Afraid my hands would pass
right through your body like
I'd just
    dreamed
        you up.

God, you were beautiful.
(Chest still hurts to think about it.
Give me a dance, starshine.
Moonlight. Melted-comet smile.)

ii.

Softness never had a meaning
until I found it in your arms.
The day you held my hand,
every poem dripped with
wisteria. Every poem smiled
at me with
     your eyes.

That was the day I started
writing all over my arms
and pretending that you were
tracing over the words with
the tips of your fingers.

That was the day I started
leaving the lights on through
     the nights.

iii.

The first creature that heard me
whisper your name like a treasure trove
was the moon.

Then the trees—the flowers—
the early morning sky bloodshot
with hunger / with want / with
your lipsticks.

Your name fit into my mouth
like it had always belonged there.
Under my tongue, gently nuzzling
the insides of my cheeks,
laughing against my lips.

iv.

Your name
    fit into my mouth
        better than my own ever has.

Like I was
    born to speak it.

Bombs & Blood & Pretence

I've been gutting words for too long,
pulling out bombs, guns, knives. I want
to do something different. *Tired of
destroying?* No. I have never known
how to destroy. They said it was my
biggest weakness. *What then?* Tired
of my hands tapping the same rhythm
daily. Tired that my hands have been
so restless these days. *Was there a
time when they weren't?* Yes. There
was a time when they could hold love
without fumbling and dropping it.
What happened? I watched the
anxiety replicate and divide and
spawn and didn't say a word until
it spread down to my lungs. *And
the love?* See-saw love. Waning-
moon love. Grew smaller as the
anxiety grew larger. Anxiety
swallowed it with a laugh and
put its claws in my chest. I said,
'maybe this is love.' Hands started
shaking and shaking like they
were an earthquake. I stood waiting
for the tsunami and said, 'maybe
this is love.' *What else?* I dance
with the lonely every night and
say, 'maybe this is love.' Nothing
else has stayed around for so
long, anyway. Maybe this is love.

The Lifecycle of a Butterfly

I went to a tulip garden yesterday
    and the blackbird in my chest
chittered so loudly I unlocked
    my skin for it.

      The opening is something
    I have forgotten how to do.
   Baring feels like LIGHTNING
on a clear day, trust like hands
    pressed flat against an electric fence.
      Trust feels like a foreign tongue,
       like my mother's voice
    when I heard it crack for the first time.

There's something brave about love.
    About unwrapping your breath and
placing it in
    someone else's hand.
When I go to sleep beside you,
    I don't think about the
jackhammer heart that refuses
    to stop SPRINTING, or about
      the blackbird with its
    beak glued shut.

I don't think about how hard it is
    to give you
      myself
    in slivers.
I just do it.

Here's me touching the knife and
    kissing the hurt.
Here's me tasting want for the first time.
        Here's me caressing freedom.
Here's me gutting my body for you.

        The opening is something I am learning.
I am still learning how to uncover
        each part of me and press it
            into your hands, saying,
here, here,
    this is me,
        here I am,

I want you to see me
and love me still.

        I want you to see me
    and know that I've never known
how to make myself visible before.

A Blurred Schema

My contacts fell out the other night
because I was crying and I hadn't put
them in properly, and it was fine,
it was fine, until I was in the backseat
of the car and the lights were flashing past—
except they looked more like blurs than
lights and for that one second I remembered
what it felt like to have you around.

Nothing concrete.
Just a blur.
Just out of reach,
always just visible but never truly there.

Sometimes my body feels like a blur, too.
Like a lie. This whole poem has been a lie,
actually. I wasn't crying and only one contact
came out, but somehow that was even worse.

I could see the lights when I closed one eye
and only blurs when I closed the other,
and I came home with a pounding headache.

So I guess what I'm trying to say is—
I've started wearing glasses more often now.
I talk to the blurs and make them my friends.
On the days you don't come home we kiss
like the marble floors of museums are
buried in our stomachs.

On the days you don't come home I stare
at the lights for hours and then I
turn them off.

Love Song from the Girl with the Bellow Lungs

i.

why do you keep
trying to save me?
don't you see
that i don't
want
to be saved?

that when you
tell me
i will be okay
i cut myself
on your words
because i
am okay being
not okay?

because it took
me long
enough
to realise that?

ii.

that day we went
to the beach you
introduced me to
all your friends &
i smiled and laughed
when i thought that
was the right reaction.

when we were alone
again you asked me
why i didn't
talk to them more.
as though talking
should be something
that comes to me
as easily as breathing.

i went home that day
and cried for hours,
beat my fists against
the mirror until
the glass
ran together
with my tears.

iii.

don't you see how
hard speaking is for me?
how hard
breathing is?

don't you see that
i am negative space
cut from the
universe and
when you ask
me to breathe
i am trying to
will myself
into
being?

iv.

i am too small
for this love.

i am too small
for my
own skin.

somedays i wake
and cannot
find myself
in my
body anymore.

i'm sorry
my chest
collapses
when you touch me.

i'm sorry that
'okay'
has become
such a
foreign
concept.

Mirages

You were a city I never got to see.
A flight that never took off (me,
clutching the wheels in bewilderment).
A star that fell and fell until I
realised it was a bomb.

Too late.
                    Too late.

Debris flying everywhere,
shrapnel and hurt buried in skin.
I thought I could forgive you
for loving me, but it turns out
you can't forgive someone for
something they didn't do.

I thought I'd forgive the sun for
rising daily, but it turns out
that would mean I'd have to
forgive myself for waking up
with it, and I don't know
how to do that.

Far away there's a city where
the children laugh and the girls
fall in love with each other,
but it disappears every time
I get on the plane.

Detonating / Detonator

Months settling between us
like dust motes, beautiful only
when looked at just the right way.

The rest of the time, it's
lying on a train track with my
skin the wrong way around.
Metal pressed to the insides
of my cheeks, gravel digging
into the small of my back. It's
your voice being poured onto
my flesh like acid. It's lips
bloodied from teeth slicing
into them.

You glorious ocean.
Hands full of sunlight.
How you haunt my days &
bed my dreams.
How you scream through
all the weeks I convinced
myself you meant nothing.

I said I wouldn't, but—
knock on my door & I'll
still fall over my feet for you.
Still hold out my arms for you.
Still dive headfirst into
your eyes.

You shattered star /
falling comet /
writhing blackhole—

take me down with you.

Atlantean

Somedays
    I tremble so hard

you take off your hands
    and leave them behind
            for me to clutch onto.

            When you come home,
            you take mine and wear
            them until the tremors pass.

    Here is a formal apology
        for all the times

    I forgot to give you your hands back.

For all the times I dumped my ache
    on you and never returned from the

bottom of the river.

    (Throw my pulse out, if you wish—
        it never was an easy weight to hold.)

Inevitability

This story is called
How It'll End.
It's also called
How I Do Not Want It To End,
or maybe,
Please Don't Let This End.

This lioness-growl heartbeat.
This blood-in-hair hunger.
This quiet desperation &
loud sadness.

All the ways of saying
I LOVE YOU
that never seem enough
when you're around.

You glance at me &
my entire spine undoes itself,
vertebrae popping out like
I'm losing teeth all over again.

It's just—
I want so many things,
and all of them begin with you.

There are so many good things
in this world,
and every one starts and
ends in your eyes.

Haunted House Hearts

Hands that feel like paperweights.
A windowless room with the
windows boarded up.
Ankles stitched on too loosely,
feet always clammy,
legs never quite feeling right.

The fear like a wild animal
when I look at you.
The nibbling at my insides,
the blood pooling at the
bottom of my ribcage.

This ache is getting repetitive,
but I guess what I'm trying
to say is that I'm too scared
to love you / that the fear
refuses to let go.

It's like—I'm terrified of ghosts,
and your body is a haunted house.
It's like—I touch you and spiders
skitter down my spine.

I don't know
how to make this hurt less.
I don't know how to make
myself less scared, how to
leave the fear behind
without feeling like I've

burnt down the only home
I've ever had.

I guess one day your arms
could feel like returning from a war,
but right now, The Fear is a war
I am too happy to lose.

Some days it puts up a white flag
and I attack anyway. I don't know who to
be without it. I don't know who I am
when I am not trembling.

Interrogating the Silence

— a conversation with a past lover

Hello. I thought you would never come back.
*But I never left. That's a lie. Okay then, I
did leave. But you were with me. Always
on my mind. That's a lie, too. Fine. What
do you want me to tell you?* Tell me
you missed me. Tell me you thought about
me at least once. Tell me you wish you'd
stayed. *I could, but they'd all be lies.*
You've never missed me? *No.* Okay.
What else do you want me to tell you?
Something. Anything. *I'm going to leave
you again.* I know. *Are you going to be
upset?* Does it matter? You'll leave anyway.
*You know, I can't leave when I'm not
actually here in the first place.* Please.
Please what? Please let me have this.
Oh. You loved me. Love. *What?* Not loved.
Love. I love you. I love you. *Oh.*
Don't you have anything to say to that?
Not really. It doesn't change anything.
But I hurt so much when you left—
I know. You're not sorry? *No.* Okay.
Can you—
[rustling, like a tissue being pulled to pieces]
Can you tell me what she's like?
*Holy. She says my name like it's
a prayer, like if she didn't say it she
wouldn't be able to stay alive. It's beautiful,*

but it's not the most beautiful thing
I've ever heard. Oh? *Ask me.* Okay.
What's the most beautiful thing you've
ever heard? *Your heart breaking.*
Quick and delicate and beautiful,
like wind chimes.

Maelstrom

always holding promises between my lips.
always holding care in the pulse at my throat.
always baring it towards you.
take it. take it.

there's so much of it here anyway.
my fingers are spinsters,
making and making that trembling
ache in my chest even when i tell
them to
stop,
that i have nowhere to put all this tender.

the other day i wrote a poem about
how your existence is the thing i'm
most grateful for, and they
called it sweet.

truth is, i have no one to give the
poems to. instead, i hold them all in my
ribcage until i can't breathe around them.

truth is, when i write poems to a 'you,'
i never know who i'm writing to, but
they're always titled:

WISHFUL THINKING.

Startold

Listen, here's what you need to do:
pretend my heart is a piñata and
punch right through it.

I'll laugh, because that's what it
says on the script. You apologise
and I'll wave it aside, saying,
no, no, this is what I was
built for, I was meant for the
hurt, for the blood embedding
itself in my skin like broken glass.

What a stupid girl I am.
How desperate to hide
the loneliness, even if only
in the toenails of a boy
who never loved me.

No, don't reply.
Follow the script.

Look me in the eye and tell
me I stink of hunger, of
everything wet and wild
and desperate.

When Cronus swallowed
his children whole, he was calling
my name.

Love & Other Unsolved Mysteries

I thought if I said 'heartbreak'
enough times, it would sound
like 'love,' but apparently it
doesn't work like that.

I wouldn't know.

I've only ever leapt away
when happiness approached—
a deer caught in headlights,
or maybe a dog with its
leg bleeding in a trap.

Only ever knowing how to gnaw at itself.

I'm sorry I flinch when you say you care.
Sorry I turn myself bullet
when you try to touch my hand,
sorry I go wolf when
you give me broken teeth.

I'm sorry I don't know how to
handle being looked after, that
I don't know what to do with all this love.

I'm sorry that when you say 'love,' I always hear
'heartbreak.'

Time, Turning

I'm writing the chapter where
you're still in love with me.
Where you open my ribcage
like it's a door (it is, for *you*)
and fall asleep beside my heart,
all curled up and breathing softly.

This is the part where we trail
across the letters and paragraphs
together, your fingers heavy on
the Gs and the Os and the Ds yet
light as feathers when they skitter
down my spine. My spine,
curved to fit the imprint of
your hand. My spine, curved
to fit into your words
(murmured into the crook of
my neck, your head nestled
in my hair—*I love you I
love you I love you*).

I'm writing the chapter where
you're still in love with me,
but then the chapter ends &
I turn the page.

THREE

All the Words I Refuse to Say

There's this ache in my chest
that I keep trying to write,
but there are some things that just
cannot be put into words.
The moonlight, for example.
Or the way the birds sound
when you wake up in the
morning despite thinking
the past night would
be your last.

This is what I can say:
my body hurts.
In the mornings the sun is a
cheese grater I am too slow
to escape from.
Every poem I've ever written is a
flushed-cheek-girl poem.
Every poem I've ever written is a
tsunami held-in-a-hand poem.
Every girl I've ever loved was a
chainsaw song, a hummingbird growl.

My body hurts,
but I cannot explain how.
Some things are just unexplainable.
The feeling of being loved,
for example. Or of not
feeling lonely.

The sound of laughter
swooping from your lover's belly
to yours.

[...]

You're right—
this is becoming a wish list.
A letter to Santa I mail every year
and sign it with anyone's name

but my own.

[Redirecting]

i.

hey, are you okay?
it's been a while since
we've talked and i guess
i just want to know
how you ar—   [DELETE]

hi, this isn't a call
out or anything,
except it kind of is.
i don't know what's
happening with you
and that's sort of concer—   [DELETE]

i'm really worried.
please get back to me
when you're fr—   [DELETE]

hey. you haven't been
around lately, is everything
alright? your friends say
they've tried contacting
you multiple times and
you never resp—   [DELETE]

so—do you want us to stop calling?   [REPLAY]
so—do you want us to stop calling?   [REPLAY]
so—do you want us to st—   [DELETE]

ii.

tongue a swollen water balloon
in the middle of my mouth.
teeth playing the role of stalagmites,
ready to pierce into anything
soft. i offer myself to my monsters,
wrists exposed & throat waning.
it's easy to go willingly when there's
no one left to stay for. when the phone
just suddenly stops ringing one day.
when you have no one to blame for it
but yourself.

i just don't feel like me anymore, &
it's not fair to answer the phone when
the person they're looking for is no longer
in this body. when the girl they all used
to love looks more wolf than girl now.

i want to say that i'm sorry,
but she's eaten even the ache.

iii.

this is the last call,
i promise,
i just want you
to know that
we all love you
and we really
hope you're oka—   [DELETE]

An Intensive Guide on How to Fail at Failing

I woke this morning with
my heart beating against
the backs of my knees.
My body has become a
forgotten paradise, a
treasure trove of
unshared memories, a
catalogue of mistake
after mistake. I break
in all the wrong places.
My spine notched up
my arms, my elbows
buried in my stomach.
My tongue rattling in
the depths of my brain.
Turns out I can't even
become a tragedy right.

The Vanishing Act

These days I can see right through my body
when I'm standing in front of a mirror.

Not existing. Non existence.
Existence-less.

When I wake in the mornings,
my body remains lying on the bed.
When I speak I see my
mouth move,
but the voice is not mine.

This morning I sat staring at the
clouds for almost an hour, and
every single one looked like
a broken heart.

Blues look like sadness now.
Reds like a warning sign.
Yellows like hunger.
Greens like desperation.

See, it's not that I hate my body,
or that I love it.

I just don't think my body is
consequential enough
for me to feel anything about it.

You know?

Inescapable

— or, I'M SORRY I TALK ABOUT THIS ALL THE TIME
BUT THERE'S NOTHING ELSE TO TALK ABOUT

I WANT TO GET
OUT OF HERE
I NEED TO GET
OUT OF HERE

TO RIP MY BODY APART
AT THE SEAMS / TO
LEAVE IT BEHIND
AND JUST RUN AND
RUN AND RUN

I'M A GIRL WHO'S
FORGOTTEN HOW
TO BE HUMAN /
HOW TO WEAR HER
OWN SKIN RIGHT /
HOW TO EXIST
INSIDE HER BODY

I WANT TO LEAVE
EVERYTHING BEHIND
EVEN IF FOR A DAY

BUT I RUN AND MY
FEET ALWAYS FOLLOW

SO HERE'S THE TRUTH:

I DON'T KNOW

I JUST DON'T KNOW ANYMORE

A How-To on Disappearing

No one understands the way we break.
Not jagged. Not knife sliding between ribs.
Not the spine, cracking.

That would be too easy.

That would be being able to know that
you're broken. That would be X-rays
showing the gaps, the fissures.
Clean breaks are easier to heal.
We do not break cleanly.

We break without breaking.
Not a crack, but a fog.
We dissipate.
Body here one moment and
not here the next.

Hands working one moment and
a dead weight the next.

We watch ourselves turn
colourless. Watch ourselves
become invisible / invincible.

This way, at least the pain is our own.
That's what I wanted all along, I guess.

Lessons in Loss

Today, a heart riddled in grief.
Hurt is a nameless child with
an empty space for a heart,
staring at the wall with
deadened eyes. Mother
lights candles and then
keeps lighting them,
unwilling to believe
that DARKNESS is a
word that exists. Unwilling
to forget what the light
looks like. The day my
family first lost someone
who truly mattered to us,
we cracked like a glass
vase being thrown onto the
floor. Even now, despite
the laughter, I could swear
some of the pieces are
still missing. Even now,
despite all the years, a
ghost knocks from behind
every eye. I have forgotten
what being whole feels like.
We all have. The ache is
too familiar, the sadness
a repeated taste on the tip
of our tongues. The world
is so heavy, but somehow,

sometime along the way,
we got used to the weight.

The Psychology of Pain

Give an example of an observational design.

> The day my aunt died, my mother cried
> for hours and I screamed at everyone
> who tried to talk to me.
> The relationship between death and grief.
> The relationship between loss and the Lost.

Give an example of an experimental design.

> Lashing out at myself versus lashing out at others.
> My reaction versus theirs.
> The way my body would shrivel up on itself
> out of fear every time I felt sad.
> The way the people around me left one
> after the other because saying 'goodbye'
> was easier than saying 'I'm still here.'

What is a within-subject design?

> Exposing a subject to all levels of the treatment.
> For example: when the hurt got too much,
> it was the hiding. Then the clawing.
> Then the praying. Then the losing
> belief. The screaming. The sudden silence.

And a between-subjects design?

Each subject exposed to a different treatment.
For example: the day my best friend fell in
love with her boyfriend, I sat with my back
against the door and cried because I
only ever knew how to say 'please stay.'

Because regardless of how many times
I repeated it (over and over and over),
no one ever did.

Chestful of Ache

That was the year we all lost something.

Dead men gurgle in their coffins, hands
to their mouths or folded across their chests,
eyes wide & open.
Staring & unseeing (like my granddad).
Sunken cheeks.
Insects in eye sockets.

Mothers wipe their hands across their shirt
fronts & wonder when the child
they loved became a monster.
A monster that talked & moved
like their child did, but
snapped & cried & cringed
like a dead thing come back to life.

The children-turned-monsters agree.
They feel soiled, buried, rotten. Like if
they move too much they will displace
the cobwebs taking root in their hearts.

No one knows what to do with all this empty.

With all the talk of monsters, no one mentioned
that sadness would create the largest ones.
With all the talk of horror, no one mentioned
that grief would claw at our insides until we'd
barely recognise the carcass in the mirror.

We've started to look at ourselves with terror.

The children want to destroy this hungry, angry,
growing thing in them, but it's becoming
harder to separate that thing from who
they were Before.

So they live with it / become better at hiding it /
start pretending that the year it all went wrong
never really existed.

It's easier that way, anyway.

Wishes & Fruit Stains

An early morning sunrise that bruises
the sky a peach-skin orange.

The crook of her throat, warm and soft
and smelling of roses and vanilla.

My mother's laughter like honeysuckle.
My mother seeing herself not as a
mistake but as a landscape of cherry trees.

A chest full of flowers. Opened, key
missing. Who ever wants to hide
happiness, anyway?

My father meaning his smiles. My
father's past, rewritten in crayons—
raspberry red love, purple plum care &
peach pit families feeding kiwifruit
green kisses.

My wrists, unscarred. My wrists,
sprouting violets. My wrists, dripping
lavender, or maybe a loud cacophony
of wisteria.

Her hand reaching out towards me.
My hand stretching towards her. The
featherlight touch of fingers, and then—

[Unsure]

My body has always been
          a question mark,

      never quite knowing what it means

          to be alive.

Smoke Stacks and Tight Chests

This morning I got out
of bed and suddenly
I felt like I was choking
(on the world /
on my future /
on the orange sky /
on every person
who said they cared).

I brushed my teeth
then crawled right
back into bed again.

That's it.
The relief was poetry.

FOUR

Moon Landings That Never Happened

The messages pile up.
The worry knocks at
my door, louder & louder.
More calls from the therapist.
Pills that should have been
taken lie scattered across the floor.
The moon taps at my window.
Stars spell out their concern.

I pretend I do not see.

For the Boys with Hungry Mouths

I watch you kiss the Sky and try
to swallow my jealousy.

You always wanted the world.
You always wanted to swallow the blue.

When you go to sleep, I touch the Sky.
Her endless, her vast, her infinite.

He will eat you up, I say.
Be careful.

Sky smiles a little sadly, nods.
Hands smaller than a buttercup's.
Says she'll be okay, that even if
you take her blue she has her
pinks, her purples, her oranges.

One day the sunrise turns and turns
but the sun never rises.
The Sky stays pink.
Stays purple.
Stays orange.

In my dreams I see an endless
(vast, infinite) blue—crying.

To the Wanderers / The Unsouled

The night called me yesterday,
called me & handed me its
stars one by one, a starfish
pulling its own limbs apart.

Called me & gave me Distance
wrapped in newspaper. Like
a perverse gift I thanked
with my tears.

Called me & threw me a
life-sized atlas of the world,
put me in the smallest corner
that was possible to exist in.

Said, '*find your way out now.*'

Hung up.

Distance: the space between her
heart & mine.

Distance: the space between my
heart & my body.

The night called and said, '*find
your way out now,*' and I'm trying.

I'm still trying.

Stagnation

And suddenly,
at one point,
everything
becomes stagnant.

The water stops
running. Glitches
instead, gurgling like
its throat has been cut.

I wake and dust
is piling on the clothes
in my room. Birds
chirp but the leaves
forget to turn brown.

Bodies flicker in and
out of being, and somehow
I'm running
outside, wind wheezing
in the hollows of
my lungs, alveoli
popping like
small balloons.

I'm howling
at the moon, screaming
at it to take me away,
for it to just MAKE
EVERYTHING
   DISAPPEAR.

And I don't know if
it hears me, don't
know if it'll reply,
but at that moment,

someone is there.

And sometimes, that's everything.

When Survival Does Not Suffice

This is what healing looks like:

> blooming / reaching towards the light /
> falling into the sunset / ripping wings off
> and watching as they regrow / holding
> a paintbrush between teeth and painting
> the trees a glowing, hazy pink.

And this is what healing looks like:

> nails painted with the ocean's foam /
> laughter like chocolate / a baby opening
> its eyes for the first time / the little hiccup
> when someone crying really hard stops /
> the watery smile after the last tear.

And this is what healing looks like:

> purple / twined vines & stitched hearts /
> hands clutching / a plane landing / sky
> scrapers / paper cuts healing / the
> smell of hospitals / reaching out to
> touch the stars /
>
> leaving the stars alone because there is
> enough wonder down here anyway /
> because there is enough wonder in just
> you alone anyway.

Rocket Launch

I've spent longer hanging off the ground
than walking on it.

Blood thundering to my head, a cup
made of bones with liquid sloshing inside.
Always in the clouds.
Feet just touching the earth,
as lightly and softly as a swan's whisper.
Lips always caught between Pluto's.
The kisses are cold, icy.
Sometimes when I pull away my
tongue sticks to the rocky surface.

But—they are still kisses.
Still lurch-in-your-belly,
make-your-toes-curl kisses.

There's something heady about reaching
so high when you're only expecting to fall.

Like you're taking the universe by the
throat and saying, *look, I know I
can never be as big as you, but you
sure as hell can't stop me trying.*

Like taking the sadness and wringing
it out and saying, *look, I know
you won't leave me alone, but you
sure as hell can't stop me living.*

Growth

The new shoot of a tree.
The thump of a newborn's heart.
Dandelion breath,
butterfly hands.

[Tell me to stop swallowing
love like a pill and
choking on it.]

[Tell me to stop sucking on
the end of poetry and
pretending that it will taste
like anything but blood.]

The pulse in your wrist like
homecoming. The pulse in your
wrist like a celebration.

[Tell me how to shed my skin
and grow from the inside out.]

Bottlebrush girl. Trellis girl.
Always stretching upward,
fingers grasping and grasping.

[Tell me to spit my sadness to
the ground like poison and
still grow around it.]

Open Heart Surgery in Space

Not the moon, but what it represents.

On the days I feel loneliest I climb
onto the roof and hold my hands out
towards the man on the moon.

He smiles, all soft and bone-like
and tender. Leans down towards me.
Plucks me up like out of all the
stars in the world,

I was the only one he wanted.

I sit opposite him and just listen.
Just look. The man on the moon
has a grey coat dusted in cream,

a woolly hat covering his ears.
When he says he's still cold I
cut off my hair and hand it to
him and he smiles like I'm
the first moonshine he's ever seen.

The man on the moon lets
me sleep on any crater I choose.
I pick the smallest one, the deepest.
The one where my body becomes
the most inconsequential.

The one where I feel most at home,
my skin almost buried and me
just being able to breathe.

(Always barely breathing.)

I wake up back in my bed,
hair grown again. The dust
on my eyelashes looks like the
remnants of sleep, and in the
mornings I wash it off like
nothing happened.

Baby's Breath

The sky this evening bloomed
like a broken purple flower,
like a ripped-in-half and
colour-bleeding-everywhere
flower, like a lavender only
just discovering what it means
to be a lavender.

Like a lavender only just discovering
how to fit into itself. Only just
discovering what it means
to be alive.

We are like this, too.

Belly Full of Inheritance

Where did you get your sadness from?

> I picked it up on the side of the road. It
> was bleeding and scratched and keening
> like a mangled thing, but it looked too
> beautiful for me to just walk away.

And the curl on the corner of your lips?

> That time I fell over on the playground and
> my wrist bled for the first time.
> Red and red and red.

What about the little hiccup in your laugh?

> My aunt. Her smile was like moonlight,
> her hands two little birds. Two little
> birds that flew away and left a screeching
> family behind.

And the purple-bruised anger?

> That I grew on my own, no help required.
> In my breastbone, between each finger.
> I wanted something to be mine alone, but
> I'm sorry I made something so ugly.

What about all the love? The love that
clamours and yells to be heard?

From the night Aphrodite whispered
in my ears. I still hear the pounding
of hearts in sync as though they live
in my brainstems. It makes the lonely larger.

The lonely? Where's that from?

Sadness' best friend. Sadness brought
it along and I couldn't turn it away, so
I let it multiply in my pulse instead.

And the stretch-across-your-entire-face smile?

From the people around me. Despite the
lonely, despite the sadness, despite the anger,
their smiles make the hearts Aphrodite left
behind beat faster / louder.
They make my heart beat in my chest again.

Warning: Dreaming

in my dreams, the sun does
    not
        blind me.

i leave the house (white converse
laced tight, hair tied with a ribbon)
and my body remains that.
my body
    stays
        a body.
doesn't become a shadow /
a ghost / a whisper.
my body stays
        solid.

when i trip and skin my knees,
    i bleed.

when my fingers graze skin,
    i feel it down to my bones.
(hear that?
in my dreams, I FEEL—)

other days, i leave the door open.
sunlight bounds in, a
puppy with its tail raised in the air.
the breeze flaps around my ankles
(see that? in my dreams,
i have a BODY—)
and i laugh alongside it.

in my dreams,
   happiness is not just a
word that rings hollowly in my mouth.
happiness is a cathedral
   too large for god
(see that? in my dreams,
there is a GOD—).

   in my dreams, i know what
      to do with my hands.

i do not lock them up in a
   cardboard box. i do not lock myself up
in a paper house too ready to catch on fire.

She Told Me She Wanted to Mean Something

You brave, aching creature.
Soon the hurt will stop gnawing
at your heart. Soon you'll feel
full again, brimming with so
much happiness it'll leak into
everyone you kiss.

Listen: you're gonna do
tomorrow better than anyone
can ever wear today.
You're gonna turn arrow,
turn sword, turn bloody battleground.
You're gonna come back home anyway.

What a beautiful mess you are.
A canvas of brush strokes,
the gentle sway of paint—
step away and you're a masterpiece.

Even the biggest miracles were
made from the smallest moments.

The Moon Writes Back

I'm crying.
The man on the moon
touches my cheek and says,
'it's okay.' He says,
'you did it. You're doing it.'

I say, 'no, no,
I'm not okay.'

The moon holds my hands,
softly.
Like a mother.

But you're here,
it says.
You're here.

Acknowledgements

I would like to thank my parents for their constant support and love, and for their eternal belief in me. You make this world a better place, and you make me a better person.

I would also like to thank my sister, my little starshine, for filling my heart with more love than I could have ever possibly imagined. In your own words, "love love love love."

A special and overwhelming thank you to Jai, for giving me the moon and more. For giving me everything (including the future).

To Ash, Grace, Anuja, and Kyle, for being patient and kind while I've been not-myself, and for always welcoming me with open arms when I do come back.

Thank you to Michelle and Peter at Platypus Press and Christian and Kelsey at Rising Phoenix Press, for believing in my writing and for turning my dreams into reality.

Finally, thank you to my readers, to all those who have stuck with me through thick and thin: this book is for you, and it will always, first and foremost, be for you.

About the Author

Darshana Suresh is a poet residing in New Zealand. She can most often be found daydreaming about all the worlds she would one day like to invent, and she believes in healing more than anything else. She would like you all to know that she is a little more okay than she used to be.

More of her work can be found at: darshanasuresh.tumblr.com

Check the Platypus Press website for further releases:

platypuspress.co.uk

CPSIA information can be obtained
at www.ICGtesting.com
Printed in the USA
LVHW041013020323
740706LV00008B/989

9 781999 773649